CW00890729

About the Author

Sophie has spent over half of her life abroad, living everywhere from Kenya and India to Bolivia and Vietnam. These experiences have profoundly shaped her work. Finally returning to the UK as a nineteen-year-old, Sophie's passion for writing and poetry continued to grow. Finding inspiration in the day to day, she is always reaching for the nearest notebook to write down a verse, or saving notes on her phone during the commute to work.

Trips & Tribulations:
A Collection of Poems

Sophie Harding Vivian

Trips & Tribulations:
A Collection of Poems

Olympia Publishers
London

www.olympiapublishers.com
OLYMPIA PAPERBACK EDITION

Copyright © Sophie Harding Vivian 2022

The right of Sophie Harding Vivian to be identified as author of
this work has been asserted in accordance with sections 77 and 78 of
the Copyright, Designs and Patents Act 1988.

All Rights Reserved

No reproduction, copy or transmission of this publication
may be made without written permission.
No paragraph of this publication may be reproduced,
copied or transmitted save with the written permission of the publisher,
or in accordance with the provisions
of the Copyright Act 1956 (as amended).

Any person who commits any unauthorised act in relation to
this publication may be liable to criminal
prosecution and civil claims for damage.

A CIP catalogue record for this title is
available from the British Library.

ISBN: 978-1-80074-521-6

This is a work of fiction.
Names, characters, places and incidents originate from the writer's
imagination. Any resemblance to actual persons, living or dead, is
purely coincidental.

First Published in 2022

Olympia Publishers
Tallis House
2 Tallis Street
London
EC4Y 0AB

Printed in Great Britain

Dedication

To Mum and Dad, for taking me on the adventure of a lifetime

ON THE ROAD

I'll take the bittersweet,

The rough with the smooth,

The timid hellos, the hard goodbyes—

Constantly on the move.

I'll take the bittersweet,

The old with the new,

The far-off adventures,

As the years flew.

I'll take the bittersweet,

The familiar with the foreign,

The home away from home,

Birthplace almost forgotten.

I'll take the bittersweet,

The close with the faraway,

The moments I wished I could stay,

Precious memories gathered along the way.

Sophie Harding Vivian

BORROWED TIME

Lingering glances, a half-smile,

Hoping you'll stay awhile.

Hushed voices, an electric force,

Always knowing this will run its course.

Holding on to draw out the seconds,

A goodbye so near it beckons.

Why so short lived? So fleeting?

What's to stop this heart from beating?

It was short, but boy it was sweet.

Moments shared in the Mekong heat.

A teenage story for the ages,

A passage to commit to life's pages.

Sophie Harding Vivian

VALLE DE LA LUNA

Everything felt alien,

The language, the lack of air,

The predicament we found ourselves in—

Feeling neither here, nor there.

But what beauty grew from the rubble.

The testing times, the initial struggle,

Soon burst like a soapy bubble—

And my love all but doubled.

Cloudless skies of the brightest blue,

The towering Andes in full view.

Fragrant Kantuta covered in dew,

Pachamama's rich tapestry novel and new.

A gateway to the sun, a valley for the moon,

Incan ruins bathed in the light of noon.

Panpipes playing a Beatles tune,

Goodbye came far too soon.

Everything felt mystical,

The language, the lack of air.

A special kind of whimsical,

My soul firmly tethered there.

Sophie Harding Vivian

ODE TO HANOI

You were a place of firsts.

First drinks and first kisses,

Bad decisions and near misses.

Walks around the lake,

Battling it out — whatever it takes.

How I wish I'd just let it ache,

So much time saved — a clean break.

Oh, I know why the caged bird sings,

The beauty that Atwood's prose brings.

Relief and refuge as the bell rings,

English class where I found my wings.

You were a place to grow—

A place of the highest highs and lowest lows.

You were home,

And no matter where I roam,

A piece of my heart is forever on loan.

Sophie Harding Vivian

FRAGMENTS

You'll find me in the frangipani,

Dancing through monsoon rains.

You'll find me in the footprints,

Marking red Saharan plains.

You'll find me in Lodhi Gardens,

Playing a game of hide and seek.

You'll find me in the terraced hills,

Gazing with wonder from peak to peak.

You'll find me in the sea of bikes,

Weaving through a bustling street.

You'll find me in the hum of cicada,

Cutting through the searing heat.

Like ashes I am scattered,

You'll find parts of me everywhere.

Sophie Harding Vivian

NO LONGER

I no longer find your structure unique, your views
impressive.

Yours is an old, tired mass in an oppressive and polluted
skyline.

Your windows a facilitator of unwanted noise and unsightly
sights.

Oh, how feelings soon evolve and change.

Exciting beginnings quickly forgotten.

A first love affair relinquished for another.

I dream of green, open spaces — of peace and quiet.

Of sunshine streaming through French doors, agape.

Of long country walks and friendly neighbours.

I no longer find you liberating, or a canvas for my expression.

I find you limiting and restraining,

Walls closing in as we attempt to grow.

You no longer have space for us,

It is time for us to go.

Sophie Harding Vivian

CRYSTAL BLUE

Crystal blue reminds me of you.

Of walks long overdue,

Of a glistening lake view,

Of a hydrangea's rare hue—

Treasured moments for two.

Sophie Harding Vivian

WHAT NOW?

What now?

Now the meticulous planning and anticipation is over.

What now?

Now the confetti has settled, vows taken.

What now?

Now our skin, once kissed by the African sun, has faded.

Step back to when life didn't revolve around one day.

Sit back and revel in the wonderfully ordinary.

While most days will pale in comparison,

The many simple, happy fragments can make up a whole.

An uninterrupted weekend — just the two of us,

Making plans over a perfectly formed flat white.

Painting a picture of our dream home, wall by wall,

Hands intertwined over a crisp bottle of Gavi.

Be present and look ahead, not back.

Reminisce and relive, but don't wallow.

For what is life if you are absent from the here and now?

Sophie Harding Vivian

REACH

Reach for the stars,

For there are none too bright,

Too far, too high,

Too out of reach.

You taught us to shine,

That we'll all have our time,

To dance among the constellations,

To make the most of life's destination.

You taught us to soar,

To pick a path we adore.

To find our own way,

To seize each and every day.

Reach for the stars,

For there are none too bright,

Too far, too high,

Too out of reach.

Reach for the stars, you said.

Then anything is possible.

Sophie Harding Vivian

HOPELESS DREAMER

Like water, I make space for everything around,

Pouring into this mould without a sound.

Like a machine on a conveyor belt — oh, how to strive?

On autopilot, an insignificant bee among the crowded hive.

Oh, how to give up the mundane for the beautifully ordinary, to appreciate the small things and not the monetary.

Oh, to throw out the mindless commute for a path less travelled, to grab life by the reigns before it unravels.

Sophie Harding Vivian

STUCK IN A MOMENT

Stuck in a moment,

As if frozen in time.

Unable to move,

To reclaim what is mine.

The hours are stagnant,

But somehow the days fly by,

Slowly losing my grasp,

As future plans turn awry.

Sophie Harding Vivian

PUSH & PULL

The push and the pull,

The role to fulfil.

To please and appease,

To sit back and to cease.

For true colours to fade,

To be kept in the shade.

The push and the pull,

The role to fulfil.

To be left on the fringes,

Holding on by the hinges.

For a watered-down self,

An object placed on the shelf.

The push and the pull,

The role to fulfil.

To bite my tongue,

Even as the words stung.

Sophie Harding Vivian

YOU ARE

You are the light in my eyes on the dullest of days,

A silver lining shining through even the thickest haze.

You are my glass half full when it should be empty,

My guide to the bright side when troubles are plenty.

You are the calm in the chaos.

Sophie Harding Vivian

FIRE OF TIME

Holding on, but hope is fading.

Fighting on, but strength is waning.

Dreams and plans up in smoke,

Fallen branches ready to stoke.

Clinging on, but barely.

Carrying on, but warily.

No phoenix rising from the ashes,

A waiting game until it caves and crashes.

In constant limbo, an endless tug of war,

Burden upon burden, weighted to the floor.

Sophie Harding Vivian

JOSHUA TREE

Take me to Joshua Tree,

To days wild and free.

To towering Yucca and glistening sand—

The sun setting in the palm of my hand.

Take me to Joshua Tree,

To a far and distant reality.

To otherworldly sights and wide-open skies—

First row seats to watch the full moon rise.

Sophie Harding Vivian

THE IN BETWEEN

What ifs and maybes,

What might have been.

Amounting to nothing, or everything?

Or something in between?

Overthinking, dwelling—

My biggest vice.

Constantly searching,

Always thinking twice.

Perhaps, potentially,

What might have been.

Insignificant, or life-changing?

Or something in between?

Theorising, speculating—

An impossible vice.

Looking for answers,

Or just the roll of a dice.

Sophie Harding Vivian

FORGET ME NOT

When days feel like every other,

When one month blends into another,

Remember sunshine on your face,

The comfort of a favourite place.

When mornings all feel the same,

When weeks start to drain and strain,

Remember treasured snapshots in time,

Living for the moment — no reason or rhyme.

Sophie Harding Vivian

PEACE

Let it go,

Let it ebb and flow.

Set it free,

Just let it be.

In the light of morning,

Salute the sun for a new day is dawning.

Live each day as if without warning,

Constantly evolving and forming.

In the dark of night,

Look to the stars for they shine bright.

For it is your story to write and rewrite,

Destined to set the world alight.

Let it go,

Let it ebb and flow.

Set it free,

Just let it be.

Sophie Harding Vivian

COUNTING GAMES

Close my eyes and count to ten,

Can't believe we're here again.

The ups and downs — the in between,

Pining for a change of scene.

Close my eyes and count to ten,

Breathe and set my words to pen.

The highs and lows — the flat line,

Searching for a guiding sign.

Close my eyes and count to ten,

Find the strength to start again.

The hopes and fears — the white lies,

Waiting for the dawn to rise.

Close my eyes and count to ten,

Can't believe we're here again.

Sophie Harding Vivian

HALCYON DAYS

May days, the heydays.

Dappled sunlight, flowers in bloom,

Radio blasting a favourite tune.

Sunscreen kisses, pastel skies,

Pausing to watch the fireflies.

These are the halcyon days.

The golden, glory days.

The days we basked in the moment.

Sophie Harding Vivian

Printed in Great Britain
by Amazon

78687311R00025